# GYMNASTICS

## Arlene Worsley

**WEIGL PUBLISHERS INC.**

**Published by Weigl Publishers Inc.**
350 5th Avenue, Suite 3304, PMB 6G
New York, NY 10118-0069

**Library of Congress Cataloging-in-Publication Data**

Worsley, Arlene.
    For the love of gymnastics / Arlene Worsley.
    p. cm.— (For the love of sports)
    Includes index.
    ISBN 1-59036-386-8 (hard cover : alk. paper) —
    ISBN 1-59036-387-6 (soft cover : alk. paper)
1. Gymnastics—Juvenile literature. I. Title. II. Series.
GV461.3.W67 2006    796.44—dc22    2005026966

Printed in the United States of America

1 2 3 4 5 6 7 8 9 10 09 08 07 06

**Cover:** Gymnasts require strength, flexibility, and balance
in order to perform well.

**Editor**
Frances Purslow
**Cover and page design**
Terry Paulhus

# Contents

# All about Gymnastics

**G**ymnastics is one of the oldest sports in the world. In Ancient Greece, children learned it in school. The Greeks believed that it was important to exercise the body as well as the mind. Gymnastics was also used to train warriors and athletes in Ancient Greece.

There are over 4,000 gymnastic clubs and about 3 million recreational gymnasts in the United States.

Friedrich Jahn, a teacher in Germany, created modern gymnastics in 1811. He invented some of the equipment used in the sport. In 1896, the first modern Olympics were held in Athens, Greece. Gymnastics was one of the nine sports that were included. Gymnastics became a more popular sport in the 1970s. It is now one of the most popular summer Olympic sports.

There are three styles of gymnastics. They are artistic, rhythmic, and trampoline. Artistic gymnastics was introduced into the Olympics in 1896. Artistic gymnasts use equipment and mats in their routines.

Rhythmic gymnastics first appeared in the Olympic Games in 1984. Rhythmic gymnasts use balls and ribbons. They also perform to music. Sixteen years later, trampoline gymnastics were brought to the Olympics. Trampoline gymnasts do difficult flips, twists, and rolls as they bounce in the air. All three types of gymnasts must be strong and **flexible**.

Boys and girls of all ages enjoy gymnastics. Very young children like to do forward rolls. As young gymnasts grow, they learn more complex skills to match their age and abilities. Gymnastics is part of the physical education program in many elementary schools. Many high schools and colleges offer competitive gymnastic programs.

Athletes combine strength with style in their routines. Gymnastics is both a sport and an art.

# Getting Started

**G**ymnasts wear stretchy, close-fitting clothing for safety and freedom of movement. Girls and women wear one-piece suits called leotards. Boys wear white, sleeveless shirts with stretchy shorts or pants. Boys wear long pants for certain events. These events are the pommel horse, parallel bars, horizontal bar, and rings. Boys wear shorts for the vault and floor exercise. Before and after performing, gymnasts wear tracksuits to keep their muscles warm. In competitions, team members wear matching uniforms.

Other gear is required to help reduce injury. Chalk powder keeps hands from slipping on the bars. Some gymnasts wear slippers, although most gymnasts prefer bare feet.

Rhythmic gymnasts have a different set of gear. They use ribbons, balls, hoops, ropes, and clubs in their routines. They also wear half-shoes. Half-shoes cover only the toe and ball of the foot.

Long hair must be tied back.

Leotards are stretchy to allow gymnasts to move freely.

**W**hen gymnasts work hard during practice or events, they **perspire**. Sweating helps the body cool down.

Gymnasts keep a towel in their bag. They use it to wipe sweat from their face and hands. They also have a water bottle filled with water. Water helps replace lost fluids due to sweating. Drinking plenty of water prevents **dehydration**.

Gymnasts need to drink water
to keep hydrated and stay healthy.

Gymnastic slippers are worn by some gymnasts.

Hand grips help prevent blisters. Blisters can form when skin rubs against bars or rings.

# The Gymnasium

Gymnasts need plenty of space to run, jump, and do flips, so their events take place in gymnasiums. Most gymnasiums are large with high ceilings. Gyms provide space for equipment and mats. Sometimes a platform is set on top of the gym floor with a layer of small springs between. These springs help gymnasts perform spins, leaps, and tumbling **moves**. Some gyms have pits that are filled with blocks of foam. When practicing **dismounts**, gymnasts land in pits. Thick floor mats and foam pits cushion landings.

**Balance beam:** The balance beam is a wooden beam 4 inches (10 centimeters) wide and 16.4 feet (5 meters) long. It is set 3.9 feet (1.2 m) above the ground.

**Floor:** The floor mat is a large square. It measures 40 feet (12 m) by 40 feet (12 m).

**Uneven parallel bars:** The uneven bars are two flexible bars set at different heights. The bars are about 4.7 feet (1.5 m) apart. The upper bar is 8 feet (2.4 m) from the floor. The lower bar is 5 feet (1.6 m) above the floor.

**Horizontal bar:** The horizontal bar is a single steel bar. It hangs 9 feet (2.75 m) above the floor.

**Still rings:** The still rings are wooden rings attached to straps. They hang about 9 feet (2.75 m) above the floor.

**Parallel bars:** The parallel bars are two flexible bars at the same height. The bars are 6.4 feet (1.95 m) above the ground.

**Pommel horse:** The pommel horse is leather-covered. It has two pommels, or handles, in the center.

**Vault:** The vault includes a runway and a "horse" without handles. The runway is a long, padded mat. There is a springboard just before the horse. The "horse" is leather-covered. It measures 5 feet (1.6 m) long and 4.5 feet (1.35 m) high.

# Gymnastics Basics

There are many **positions** and moves in gymnastics. Body positions are one of the first things gymnasts learn. The four main body positions are the pike, straddle, tuck, and layout. These positions are used in all events. They are combined with other positions and moves to produce a routine.

Gymnasts also learn different moves. Having good balance is vital for many gymnastic moves, such as the handstand. Other basic moves include the cartwheel, **somersault**, **round-off**, and forward and backward rolls. These moves are used in many events. The run-up is a few quick steps that help a gymnast gain speed during a floor or vault event.

Most coaches start gymnasts on the floor event. Gymnasts spend many hours practicing. Floor routines combine **tumbling runs** with artistic moves. Artistic moves include the round-off, handspring, and **salto**.

The endings of gymnastic routines should be controlled. There should be little or no movement when a gymnast performs a landing, such as a dismount from the vault or bars.

The layout is a position in which gymnasts stretch their bodies into a long line that is straight or slightly arched. This can be done on a variety of equipment, including the parallel bars.

S killed gymnasts spend many hours a day practicing their routines. They have to train hard to improve their skills. A typical workout consists of three parts. They are warm-ups, **apparatus** practice, and **conditioning**.

Warm-ups are done at the beginning and at the end of a practice or performance. Gymnasts stretch, bend, and flex their bodies. It is important to stretch after the muscles have been warmed up. Stretching helps prevent injury and maintain flexibility. Some stretches include arm circles, toe touches, and neck stretches.

After warming up and stretching, gymnasts practice their routines on the apparatus. Then, the rest of the time is spent on conditioning. Conditioning includes push-ups, sit-ups, splits, and running. These activities help gymnasts increase their strength and flexibility.

Left: Pike
Below: Straddle
Right: Tuck

CHECK IT OUT

Read more about gymnastics apparatus and moves at www.umgym.com

Click on About Gym.

# Events

**A**lthough some gymnastic events are the same for boys and girls, some are different. For example, only females participate in rhythmic gymnastics.

Boys compete in six events: floor exercise, vault, pommel horse, rings, parallel bars, and horizontal bars. Girls compete in four events: floor exercise, vault, uneven parallel bars, and balance beam. Males and females have three events in common: floor exercise, vault, and parallel bars. However, there are differences in how they perform these events.

Boys and girls perform different styles of floor routines. Girls' routines are set to music. They focus on dance and tumbling. Boys' routines focus on strength, balance, and tumbling.

Gymnasts must keep the rings as still as possible during their performance.

**B**oys and girls both use the vault, but they position it differently. Boys vault over it lengthwise, while girls position it sideways.

Parallel bars for boys are set side by side. Girls compete in uneven parallel bars. One bar is higher than the other.

Only girls compete in balance beam, and only boys use the pommel horse, rings, and horizontal bar.

# Where the Action Is

It takes years of practice to become a skilled gymnast. Some gymnasts enter the sport at about eight years of age.

Most gymnastics clubs offer some programs just for fun and some for competition. These programs prepare students to perform in front of people. Gymnasts usually take lessons at gymnastic clubs. When students are ready to compete, there are many opportunities. There are about 85,000 competitive gymnasts in the United States. There are many different levels of competition.

The United States Gymnastics Foundation (USGF) sponsors gymnastic meets at the local, state, and national levels. More than 4,000 clubs in the United States offer gymnastic lessons and competitive teams. Many schools and colleges also have competitive gymnastic teams. Gymnasts compete against other gymnasts at the same level and same age group. There are many competition levels, from beginner to **elite**.

Carly Patterson won the gold medal in the artistic gymnastics individual competition at the 2004 Olympics in Athens, Greece.

**E**lite gymnasts compete at international meets and the Olympics. There are five to seven members on an Olympic gymnastics team. The U.S. national teams are chosen from 300 elite gymnasts.

Important gymnastic meets include the Olympic Games and the World Championships. Usually two judges evaluate each routine in each event. At major events, there are as many as four to six judges. Each event has a set of required routines. Routines must show creativity and must be exciting to watch.

Each routine is judged on a 10-point scale. At the Olympics, this is called a Code of Points. Points or tenths of a point are taken off for mistakes. The 10 possible points are based on the level of difficulty and the nature of the routine. Awards are given to teams and to individuals.

After a gymnast's performance in an event, each judge decides on a score. The scores are then totaled, and an average is calculated for that gymnast.

**CHECK IT OUT**

*Find out more about gymnastics competitions at*

**www.usa-gymnastics.org**

# Early Stars of the Sport

**T**he sport of gymnastics has attracted many superb athletes. They thrill fans who fill the stands or watch them on television.

## SAWAO KATO

**BORN**
October 11, 1946
**REPRESENTED**
Japan
**EVENTS**
Floor, rings, parallel and horizontal bars, pommel horse

### Career Facts:

- Sawao Kato is considered one of the most successful male gymnasts of the Olympics.
- In three Olympics, he won 12 medals. Eight of the medals were gold.
- Sawao was inducted into the International Gymnastics Hall of Fame in 2001.

## KURT THOMAS

**BORN**
March 29, 1956
**REPRESENTED**
United States
**EVENTS**
Pommel horse, floor exercise

### Career Facts:

- Kurt was the first U.S. male to be a serious contestant in gymnastics.
- He invented the "Thomas Flair," a twirling scissors move on the pommel horse.
- He won a gold medal at the 1978 World Championships.
- Kurt is the only gymnast to ever win the **Sullivan Memorial Trophy**.

## NADIA COMANECI

**BORN**
November 12, 1961
**REPRESENTED**
Romania
**EVENTS**
Balance beam and
uneven parallel bars

### *Career Facts:*

- Nadia is the first gymnast in Olympic history to receive a perfect score of 10. She was 14 years old.
- At the 1976 Olympic Games, she won three gold medals, a silver medal, and a bronze medal.
- Nadia was the first gymnast, male or female, to win a third consecutive European title in 1979.
- Nadia helped the Romanians win their team gold medal at the World Championships in 1979.

## OLGA KORBUT

**BORN**
May 16, 1955
**REPRESENTED**
Soviet Union
**EVENTS**
Balance beam, floor,
uneven bars

### *Career Facts:*

- In 1972, Olga won her first Olympic medals. She won three gold medals and one silver medal.
- She was the first person to do a backward somersault on the uneven parallel bars.
- In 1991, she moved to the United States and began teaching gymnastics.

# Superstars of Gymnastics

**G**ymnasts in the Olympics and other competitions have inspired young athletes to try this exciting sport.

## VITALI SCHERBO

**BORN**
January 13, 1972
**HOMETOWN**
Minsk, Belarus
**EVENTS**
Pommel horse, rings, horizontal bars, vault, parallel bars, floor exercise

### Career Facts:

- In the 1992 Summer Olympics, Vitaly became the first person to ever win four gold medals in one day.
- He was also the first gymnast to win six gold medals in one Olympics.
- In 1996, he won four bronze medals in the Summer Olympics.

## SVETLANA KHORKINA

**BORN**
January 19, 1979
**HOMETOWN**
Belgorod, Russia
**EVENTS**
Uneven bars, floor exercise, vault, balance beam

### Career Facts:

- Svetlana has been a World Champion in gymnastic events nine times.
- She won silver in the women's individual all-around competition at the 2004 Summer Olympics.
- Svetlana won gold medals at both the 1996 and the 2000 Olympics for uneven bars.

## CATALINA PONOR

**BORN**
August 20,1987
**HOMETOWN**
Constana, Romania
**EVENTS**
Balance beam, floor exercise, vault, uneven bars

### Career Facts:

- At age 16, Catalina won three silver medals in three gymnastics events at the World Championships in 2003.
- The following year, she won three gold medals at the European Championships.
- Also in 2004, Catalina won three gold medals in the Summer Olympics.

## SHANNON MILLER

**BORN**
March 10, 1977
**HOMETOWN**
Rolla, Missouri
**EVENTS**
Balance beam, uneven bars, floor exercise

### Career Facts:

- During her career, Shannon has won seven Olympic medals and nine World Championships.
- Shannon is the only American to win two straight World Championship all-around titles. She won them in 1993 and 1994.
- Shannon was a member of the U.S. women's gymnastics team known as "The Magnificent Seven."

# A Healthy Gymnast

**G**ymnastics requires tumbling, jumping, and other energetic movements. To do well in gymnastics, it is important to eat the right foods. Gymnasts must eat healthy foods and drink plenty of water. Gymnasts need short bursts of energy and power in their routines. Eating balanced meals builds strong muscles and helps athletes work hard. Foods from the four food groups, such as **carbohydrates**, fruits and vegetables, protein, and milk products, contain **nutrients** needed for a healthy body. Strong bones and muscles are important when performing in an active sport, such as gymnastics.

Fruits and vegetables provide vitamins and minerals to keep athletes healthy.

**E**ating too much or too little can affect a gymnast's performance. Also, eating foods that contain large amounts of sugar leads to rapid energy swings. It is important to choose foods that are easy to digest before a gymnastics event.

Athletes need to drink water to replace what they lose when they sweat. When muscles work hard, they produce heat in the body. To keep cool, the body releases heat through sweat.

Gymnasts must train very hard to maintain a body that is both strong and flexible. Eating a balanced diet helps them stay in shape.

CHECK IT OUT

Discover more about sports and nutrition at
**www.urbanext.uiuc.edu/**
*Then click on
Nutrition & Health.*

# Gymnastics Brain Teasers

**T**est your gymnastics knowledge by trying to answer these brain teasers!

**Q** Who is the "father of gymnastics"?

**A** Friedrich Jahn is the "father of gymnastics."

**Q** How many sports were featured in the first Olympics in Athens, Greece?

**A** Nine sports were featured in the first Olympics in Athens, Greece.

**Q** How many artistic events do boys compete in?

**A** Boys compete in six artistic events.

**Q** What is gymnastic equipment called?

**A** Gymnastic equipment is called apparatus.

**Q** Which Olympian was the first gymnast to ever receive a perfect score?

**A** Nadia Comaneci was the first gymnast to ever receive a perfect score.

**Q** Name the four main body positions in gymnastics.

**A** The four main body positions in gymnastics are the pike, straddle, tuck, and layout.

# Glossary

**apparatus:** the equipment used in gymnastic events

**carbohydrates:** foods that provide energy

**conditioning:** physical activities that help the body become more fit

**dehydration:** extreme loss of water from the body

**dismounts:** getting off an apparatus by landing on both feet

**elite:** very high level

**energetic:** requiring much energy

**flexible:** able to bend easily

**gymnasts:** athletes who participate in gymnastics

**moves:** certain set ways of moving the body

**nutrients:** substances needed by the body and obtained from food

**perspire:** sweat

**positions:** arrangement of body parts, or posture

**round-off:** a cartwheel move landing on both feet

**routines:** series of moves and positions

**salto:** a flip

**somersault:** a forward or backward flip in the air

**Sullivan Memorial Trophy:** an award for performance and sportsmanship

**tumbling runs:** moves in which the gymnast runs before tumbling

# Index